D1188052

First published in Great Britain 2004
By Aesculus Press
PO Box 5276
Swadlincote
Derbyshire
DE11 9ZT

A catalogue record for this book is available from the British Library

ISBN 1-904328-10-5

Photographs, with thanks to:
Breville (UK) pages: 15, 17, 19, 31, 63
Breville (AUS) pages: 11, 13
Brian pages: 59, 67, 93, 105, 109, 111, 113, 132, 133, 148
Catlin Historical Society page 10
Lindsay Butler: 97, 134, 139, 155, 41, 26-27, 28, 33, 35
Ross pages: 49, 55, 77, 85, 91, 49
Stilton Cheese Makers Assoc. 107

®MARS/®SNICKERS/®MALTESERS are registered trademarks. Recipes are not endorsed by Masterfoods

®MARMITE is registered trademark. Recipes are not endorsed by Bestfoods Ltd

Designed by Laurel Tree / Printed by Ashford Press Ltd
Help and assistance from Dan & Sal @ www.mousehouseprintshop.co.uk
Cover design James Baldwin @ www.colouring-in.co.uk

Round the world toasties

Sweet toasties

Time wasting toasties

With thanks...

WWW.TRIEDANDTOASTED.COM

PREFACE

I was given my first - and only - toastie maker on Christmas Day 1998. This hallowed machine has gone on to accompany me to university and beyond and it was while living in a bedsit in Camden, North London that I thought about writing this book. The reason? I thought of the title 'Tried and Toasted' and knew I couldn't let such a clever piece of wordplay go to waste! More importantly, I was forever eating toasties, and soon my housemates and I were experimenting with 'adventurous' ingredients and different types of bread - it seemed only natural that a book should be published recounting our findings.

Since those early days the book has become a real talking point, and it's surprising how many people have a good idea for a toastie in them, just waiting to come out. Some of the toasties here are a result of chance meetings or strange conversations in bizarre places.

And why do so many people love toasties? Because they are cheap and easy to make of course! Oh, yes - and absolutely delicious …

BEFORE WE START...

HISTORY

It was the Egyptians who began making bread as we know it today. They would leave their dough out in the scorching heat of Cairo and found it would expand to become bread. So, who thought of toasting this bread? The word toast derives from the Latin words Torrere, Tostum - to scorch or burn. The Romans introduced toasting to Britain, from where it was passed on to America.

In the late 1800's, electricity was becoming a major part of life and inventions harnessing it to make living easier swiftly followed. The electric toaster was relatively slow in development, and was invented in the last decade of that century. From 1912, Otto Frederick Rohwedder worked on bread slicing machines and, in 1928, he designed a machine that could slice and wrap the bread. While he was busy doing that, a Mr Champion, in Catlin, USA, was enthusiastically working on a project of his own and, before 1920 (although it

Mr Champion's Tostwich, 1924

was not patented until 1924) the world's first electric toasted sandwich maker was created! Champion had invented a sandwich toaster and, in a moment of inspired genius, called it a Tostwich (however toastwich would have made more sense).

How did the toasted sandwich evolve to its present state, whereby all the content is sealed in and there is a diagonal line across it? I was pondering this very topic when I stumbled upon an old article in *The Guardian* (Wednesday October 3, 2001) in which it said that Breville invented the sandwich toaster.

It would appear the Oldham-based company are responsible for the 'Cut-n-Seal' mechanism that makes the toastie what it is - which isn't a toasted sandwich. They introduced the 'Breville scissor action snack 'n' sandwich toaster' to a "responsive" UK public in the early 70's.

Still, I wanted more detail and, after further contact with Breville, I made an amazing discovery: the toastie is not

British invention; indeed, Breville was formed by two Australians. In 1932, Bill O'Brien and Harry Norville mixed their last names together and the Breville brand was created. They made radios at first, but, after the war and the arrival of the television, they turned their attentions to small appliances. After O'Brien had set up the Breville Research and Development centre in the 1960's the ideas just kept on coming, and in 1974 they hit on a real winner.

Those geniuses in the Breville Research and Development centre had found a solution to the problem of toasted sandwich spillage

1974 will be remembered for several significant events including the death of Duke Ellington, Richard 'Watergate' Nixon becoming the first US president to resign, West Germany beating Holland to win the World Cup and Australia voting for 'Advance Australia Fair' as their new national anthem. But the most noteworthy occurrence was surely the release of the 'Snack 'n' Sandwich toaster'. It was a huge hit, selling 400,000 in the first year, making it one of Australia's "most successful product launches".

Those geniuses in the Breville Research and Development centre had found a solution to the problem of toasted sandwich spillage.

Now their innovative design is used by dozens of manufacturers, but Breville are still the market leaders, with a range of 14 sandwich toasters, sold to all the major European countries and accounting for 50% of the British market.

Snack 'n' Sandwich toaster

Iconic toastie machine

TOASTIE MAKERS

You may well find yourself presented with a toastie maker by a kindly friend or relative, as a sign you are on the verge of adulthood and can be trusted with such a sophisticated machine. Be happy with it and look after it well. Due to the robust nature of this piece of equipment, there is no reason it shouldn't last your entire adult life.

If you are thinking about buying your own or giving one as a gift yourself, here is a short overview of what is available. It may be overwhelming at first, when you begin researching your prospective purchase; after all, there are many different models and designs out there. Don't panic - once you've read this you'll have a better understanding of what will best suit your needs.

Size

When buying a toastie maker, consider how often you think the user will be tucking in to a toastie and how many people they live with. This will affect the size of the machine that you purchase.

Three choices:

Single slice: The trouble with a single slice toastie machine is that toasties are so damn good you'll want two at a time - so this is a significant drawback. However, to extract a positive from the negative, while you sit down and enjoy your toastie, the second helping will be cooking nicely!

Two slice: Probably the most commonly seen design, when not deplorably hidden away in the kitchen drawer (shame on you!). This is a good machine and ideally suited to a student abode - one toastie can be made for you and another for your friend.

Four slice: Anyone who has this in their kitchen is either a member of a big family, a regular entertainer, very popular or simply a huge toastie fan! However, if you are the latter, remember that to ensure all four toasties are still hot upon consumption you'll have to eat them at record speed, which entails obvious indigestion risks.

How it looks

In a market fraught with competition, the look of a machine can be a swaying factor. Breville have introduced many 'novelty' toastie makers, including one that looked like a cow and even mooed realistically! However, these will soon be unavailable in Europe. New European law rules out such appliances, as they look like children's toys and could be dangerous.

These fun-looking toastie machines are usually single slice but some more interesting designs are found in the two slice range. Some just look quite square, others look rounded and some - like this Russell Hobbs pictured - look fantastic! The four slice machines all look either very boring and square, or remarkably like a UFO. They always manage to appear smaller than you'd imagine as well.

Feet!

If you want to slide the toastie maker around for some reason (perhaps trying to invent a new game!) then avoid a machine that comes with 'non-slip feet'.

Lights

Some toastie machines will have two lights; one that indicates the machine is on and the other to let you know when it has reached cooking temperature. I've always found the concept of waiting for optimal heat to be reached before putting in your pre-prepared toastie a strange one. In the time spent waiting for the light to go off (or on) the meal could be busy cooking while the plates are heating up. All toastie machines will have at least one light, so the decision is between one light or two.

Space

Kitchen space may be at a premium so ask yourself: "Do I require a toastie maker that has a wrap-around-cord base?" The main advantage of this is that the toastie can be stored neatly. But why in Gods name would anybody want to 'store' his or her toastie machine? Its rightful place is as the proud centrepiece of the modern kitchen.

Cleaning

Some newer toastie machines come with removable 'easy clean' plates. The idea is that the plates are removed and can then be put in the dishwasher, or piled alongside the other 'to do' washing-up. A good idea if you're of a particularly clean disposition.

Genuine

If you want a toastie that has 'Large, deep, genuine Breville cut and seal' plates then your choice of manufacturer is slashed down to one. (Breville, if you hadn't guessed.)

I DOUGHN'T BELIEVE IT!

Isn't toastie spelled toasty?

According to Microsoft Word, yes it is! However, I'm not convinced, so I'm going against MS and spelling it TOASTIE - those red under-lines will not deter me! A flick through the ever-reliable Cambridge dictionary tells us that the 'Toastie/Toasty' is "especially British ... a toasty is a sandwich that has been toasted". Conclusive evidence that toastie can be spelled either way.

Is a toastie a gaffle?

After literally minutes of extensive research, I have concluded that a toastie has many pseudonyms, including gaffle (Australia), toast (Turkey), pocket sandwich (USA) and toastie pie (USA).

Shouldn't this book be called: Tried and Toastied?

This is a very good question. If you look up 'toastied' in the dictionary you won't find anything, unsurprisingly, as the word doesn't exist. However, if you look up toasted you'd find that one definition is:

"The act of raising a glass and drinking in honour of or to the health of a person or thing."

Clearly not what I was looking for! However, another definition is:

"To warm thoroughly ... Sliced bread heated and browned."

Perfect! So that's why I've gone with Tried and Toasted. Oh, and it sounds miles better than Tried and Toastied too.

When I bite into one end of a toastie the content will invariably make its way out of the other!

There is a simple solution to this problem: use a knife and fork to eat any potential 'squirters'. This also has psychological benefits - of which more later.

If the filling is made from a slice of something - say ham - the first bite results in the entire slice being pulled out and causes terribly bad burns to the chin.

This can also be avoided by using a knife and fork. Also, cut any slice fillings up in to small pieces - things like tomato can cause serious damage if residing on one's chin!

Toasties are for cheapskates aren't they?

Not so! This book will illustrate how classy a toastie can be. Any half-decent dinner party should have a toastie starter - unless, of course, it's actually the main meal.

In 2003, a total of 1.1 million sandwich toasters were sold in the UK and throughout the 90's there was a steady increase in toastie maker sales. Breville insist: "Today, most homes will have a sandwich maker, its target market is across all ages and incomes". The 'sandwich maker' (Toastie maker/machine) breaks down the boundaries of economic and social background - it's a wonderfully all-inclusive kitchen appliance. Just for 'cheapskates'? Millions of satisfied toastie consumers will tell you differently.

"What's your comfort food? Ham and cheese toasties with tomatoes and a good grind of pepper." - Gary Rhodes, Metro Life, 2003

How many sides of the bread should be buttered?

Well, this really is a pertinent question. It is entirely up to the individual whether they want to butter the inside, outside or both sides of the bread. But it isn't necessary to butter any - if you're a busy person with a lot to do, fiddling around buttering can waste valuable time.

Buttering the outside can add to the flavour and nicely browns the toastie. But if the outside is not buttered, the toastie won't stick. It is advisable to oil the hot plates every now and again to keep them non-stick!

Also consider the content of the toastie. To butter the outside of a toastie featuring a chocolate bar could make it quite disgusting and uneatable. However a baked bean toastie, or a cheese toastie may - some would argue - increase the enjoyment and taste of the toastie. So consider your levels of idleness and the content of the toastie before buttering any surfaces.

Toastie Etiquette

Novice toastie consumers frequently embarrass themselves with shocking breaches of etiquette. But you can avoid such humiliation by adhering to this straightforward code of conduct:

You have been over-eager to eat your freshly cooked toastie and have taken a sizeable bite, only to discover the content has reached a temperature of first-degree burn-giving proportions. DO NOT PANIC. Although the upper of part your mouth may be literally aflame, it is important not to show any pain; and certainly don't lob abuse at the toastie - you took the bite and you cooked it, it's not the toastie's fault. Under no circumstances should you project the piece out of your mouth. This is a highly objectionable thing to do, and may put fellow diners off their meals. If the pain is unbearable, excuse yourself from the eating area and go to the loo to release the offending piece from your mouth.

Sometimes, when eating a toastie, the content may drip out and land on the chin. Despite the pain that may be felt, do not draw attention to it. Discreetly wipe it off your chin with a tissue/napkin/sleeve/hand. Don't ever try and lick the mark away as nobody wants to see an unsightly tongue swinging around trying to ensnare spillage.

Even more importantly, don't forget about the spillage altogether after planning to 'wipe it off later'. Imagine the embarrassment as your fellow diners stare in horror at the large blob on your chin while you calmly carry on chatting about the days events. Having expected you to sort out the spillage, they have now left it more than a minute to say anything and are left in a very awkward position. Expect any social status you have achieved to swiftly evaporate once word of such a faux pas spreads.

Health and Safety

Sharp Knife

When using a knife, ensure you are holding the right end. This is the end that is smooth and rounded, and should not feel uncomfortable to hold.

Warning:

If, when you grip the

knife, you feel a sharp pain in your hand and blood becomes visible, you are holding the wrong end.

A benefit of holding the correct end is that the ability to cut through things is significantly increased.

To cut cheese, try buying a 'cheese slicer', a marvellous invention which produces nice even slices of cheese every time.

Table Knife

The blunt cousin of the more potent 'sharp knife', already discussed. Although they are generally harmless, do not be fooled. It could still cause considerable pain if stabbed into one's eye.

Fork

When enjoying your toastie, do not get over excited and put the toastie-carrying fork too aggressively into your mouth. Not only could this result in excruciating tongue-piercing, but you may also find the fork is accidentally swallowed, with inevitably painful consequences when it exits your body at the other end.

Tins and Tin openers

This is a reliable and useful piece of kitchen equipment. Do not test the reliability or sharpness of it by placing a digit in and turning the handle.

Once a tin is open, be aware of the sharp edges that are exposed. If the tin has a peel-back lid, be very careful. Not only is there a distinct possibility of slash-back, but the lid may also spring back and separate your finger from the rest of your body.

Electricity

If you have just washed your hands, do not switch the plug on while they are still dripping wet. Either don't bother to wash your hands, or dry them before going close to any plugs. On this note, it is not recommended to use a toastie machine outside, particularly when it is raining.

Toastie maker

When a toastie maker is on, the heat of the plates is extreme. Therefore, do not put your hand in it and close the lid. And, although you may be tempted to kiss it after it has produced yet another fantastic toastie, this is a flawed idea. The outside of the machine also gets very hot. If you have just made a toastie and you see some content has leaked out, do not lick it clean or use your finger to wipe it up. It is not a mixing bowl!

When making a toastie, be sure none of the wire is caught in the machine before closing it. I'm not sure what would happen, but my well-honed instincts tell me an explosion of some kind would be on the cards.

When the toastie is on or off do not head-butt and/or kick it, even if it has annoyed you, or you haven't got a football. Also, the toastie maker should never be thrown/hurled at people. It is a solid kitchen appliance that could cause severe pain.

Leftover food

If you decide to cook a toastie with leftover food, please be conscious of the fact that not all food is suitable for re-heating. Carefully research what food you may re-heat before doing so. Failure to do this may cause your body to react the next day. Vomiting and/or severe and uncontrollable bouts of diarrhoea may be the outcome of poor food research and over zealous use of leftovers.

Bread

Ensure the bread you use in the toastie maker is not off in any way. If the bread is hard, it is not good to use. In fact, the term for this type of bread is 'stale'. Also, bread can change colour, generally to a shade of white and green. When this happens it usually has a layer of fluff on it called mould. Once again, this is not good bread to use as mould is: "furry growth of tiny fungi on a damp substance". Not very edifying, you'll agree!

How to eat your toastie

If you prefer not to use a knife and fork for this task, please read the following very carefully. A toastie's content will invariably be exceedingly hot. Fillings such as leftover pasta sauce or baked beans are highly likely to spill if the toastie does not enter the mouth at the right angle. Be sure to follow these instructions:

1 Cut along the diagonal line to separate the two sections.

2 Make perforations in the toastie to cool it down a little and get the steam out.

3 Wear a safety glove on the holding hand. This has the dual purpose of making the toastie easier to hold and also, if any of the content should spill out, the glove will act as a shield to protect your hand.

4 No matter what angle your face is at, your toastie should enter your mouth at a 45 degree angle from the ground in front of you.

Under no circumstances should the toastie enter the mouth at a 45 degree angle from the ground behind you, unless you are hunched over the toastie. ALWAYS keep the toastie pointing down.

5 When the toastie is not in the mouth, make sure the hole created by the bite is facing up. Doing this makes sure the content of the toastie remains content and does not become spillage.

6 Once the toastie is finished, wipe mouth clean of any unwanted crumbs and/or spillages that may be nestling around the mouth.

7 Wash hands and dry.

TOP TOASTIE TIPS

Knife to know you fork about it!

My housemate in Camden, Charlie, used to eat almost any snack - including sometimes crisps - with a fork. When I quizzed him as to why he did this, he claimed that, psychologically, using cutlery made him feel like a proper meal had been consumed (perhaps some scientific testing should be done on this - it could be a revolutionary new dieting technique). After pausing for a hearty laugh, I thought I'd try out this ground-breaking theory on a toastie, and I've never looked back!

So, use a knife and fork to eat your toastie. As well as benefiting from the psychological 'feel-good' factor, you will find chin-burning spillage is a thing of the past.

Egg

There is no need to pre-cook the egg; it will cook in the toastie machine. The key to a successful egg toastie is the bottom piece of bread and the size of the egg. Make sure a medium sized egg is used as if the egg is too large, the task of containing it is made much harder.

Be warned, this toastie can go extremely wrong and result in an almighty mess. If the egg starts to slip, just encourage it back into place, slap the top piece of bread on and close the toastie machine as quickly as you can.

The bottom piece of bread.

It's all in the preparation. The idea is to try and create a bowl for the egg to sit in:

1. Flatten the bread with your thumb.
2. Place in the toastie machine and softly push the bread into the toastie pouches.
3. Carefully break the egg on to the bread.
4. Season to taste.
5. Place the second piece of bread on top.
6. Close the lid of the toastie machine.
7. Remove toastie and eat!

Off-cuts

Pop along to your friendly local butcher, and politely ask for any meat off-cuts they may have. They will kindly present you with a bag filled with little pieces of meat and, for a fee, will let you walk out of the shop with them. This process can also be performed at the 'deli' counter in your local supermarket. This meat is ideal for toasties as it is already in small pieces, so you don't have to bother cutting the stuff up, and an added bonus is that it is cheaper to buy.

Herbs

Every kitchen cupboard in the land should contain herbs. Whether it's a bag of mixed herbs or a selection of herbs and spices from around the world, I guarantee they will enhance your culinary pleasure. Chilli (powder) and garlic (powder) are also worthy additions to a chef's cupboard. Put in a toastie, these seasonings can really make a difference to a 'normal' toastie. With any variety of baked bean toastie, the addition of herbs and/or chilli powder and/or garlic puree/powder will be highly complementary.

Spread um! Well, don't actually...

When having a toastie containing a sweet spread like jam, do not treat it like a normal sandwich which you are then going to toastie. In other words, do not spread the jam. It is much better to put two dollops of jam (for example) in each section of the toastie. The jam will melt and spread itself without the risk of all the flavour and taste being baked out of it.

It's all about out-saucing!

When having a toastie with sauce such as tomato ketchup, HP, chilli or Tabasco, never put the sauce inside the toastie. The main reason for this is that the flavour of the sauce is seriously lost in the toastieing process. Also, some sauces get unbeliev- ably hot and could cause real pain. I'd suggest applying the  sauce to the toastie after it is cooked or put it on the side of your plate and dip the toastie in.

I would also suggest spreads such as MARMITE are applied on the outside of a cooked toastie. However, if you want a weaker taste - this particularly applies to MARMITE - then put it in the toastie and cook.

www.
tried
and
toasted
.com

BREAD, CHEESE AND KEYS

You Breada Believe It!

"Without bread all is misery."
William Cobbett, British journalist (1763-1835)

So said the rural warrior, and I couldn't have put it better myself. I often find myself wondering what I'm going to eat, and then, there in the corner of my almost empty cupboard, I spot a loaf of economy white bread. Crisis averted! This may come as a surprise to some of you less-educated types, but there are actually many different types of bread; bread of different colours, shapes and sizes. It is for this reason that bread has to have a special mention.

Throughout this book, I encourage the reader to use two pieces of bread in most of the dishes and, unless otherwise stated, I am referring to the bog-standard white, medium-sliced, variety. This is the toastie 'industry-standard' bread for the following reasons:
Economy bread is cheap.
The slices fit perfectly into a toastie maker, unlike the 'deluxe'

bread, which requires trimming down before it goes in.
Medium-sliced bread means you can close the toastie maker without having a severe struggle on your hands, and the content of the toastie will get cooked to perfection.
Crappy white bread has no distinct taste, so is unable to detract from the flavour of the toastie.

Having said that, there are other breads that can be used to good effect. Pitta bread is very good with cheeses and makes a nice change from normal bread - croissants and bagels are classy substitutes in a cheese-based toastie as well. Most Indian breads will work wonderfully too but remember, chapati's are thin, so don't pack them too full of content and handle them with care. As a rule-of-thumb, try and use bread that isn't too thick, isn't crusty and isn't mouldy.

Brown or wholemeal bread is fine to use, but I always feel it is too heavy for a toastie, particularly if it's a quality loaf. However, this does not mean it should never be used; sometimes it can complement the content of the toastie, an example being the world renowned leftover curry toastie.

THE CHEESE KNEES

A lot of people are of the opinion that the toastie maker is only ever called into action when there is too much cheese in the house, which has to be used quickly. You'll soon find this is not the case, but it's certainly true that cheese is a classic ingredient - and therefore well worth discussing in depth.

Cheese *n.* food made from pressed milk curds; shaped mass of this.
Curd *n.* thick soft substance, esp. (*pl.*) that formed when milk turns sour.

That is what my Oxford Minidictionary has to say about cheese, which is why it's important to clarify a few things about cheese and the different types available.

To start with, eating a thick, soft substance which is basically milk gone-off is nice! It may not sound particularly appealing but is invariably darn tasty.

There are three main types of cheese: Hard, semi and soft. The categories are very good clues as to the texture of the cheese. Hard and semi are good cheeses to toastie; soft cheese has the potential to make a real mess and not really be worth it. Below is a brief guide to different types of cheese - I have not marked them as different people have their own preferences.

Cheddar When a little village in Somerset called Cheddar (Gorge) started making this cheese, I doubt they knew it would become one of the most loved cheeses in the world. This is the industry standard cheese and benefits from being cheap to buy and melting perfectly, without much loss to the flavour.

Edam Holland's second most exported cheese (behind Gouda) is a great one for toastieing. Recognisable by its red paraffin coating (yellow in Holland) this is an inexpensive cheese, which, like Cheddar, melts well and retains flavour.

Camembert A wonderfully tasty cheese on it's own, with fruit or on toast. It can be incredibly smelly and strong in taste. However, when put in a toastie it loses most of that appeal while continuing to really smell.

Red Leicestershire This is a very versatile cheese with good taste and great melting qualities.

Brie This is a soft French cheese, that is very nice on toast, but NOT in a toastie! The inside of it goes very runny (a good brie should be runny at room temperature), the rind never really melts and the flavour is lost a bit.

Double Gloucester A nice dense cheese with good flavour, which is not lost in the toastieing of it. Once upon a time this cheese only used milk from Gloucester cows but now, unfortunately, those good cows are nearly extinct, although happily their name will live on.

Stilton This great cheese is a good one to toastie. Although it does go quite runny, it is worth it due to the fact the flavour is so good. If you are on a diet, be warned: it is 45% fat due to the way it is matured!

Cheese spread Can be used.

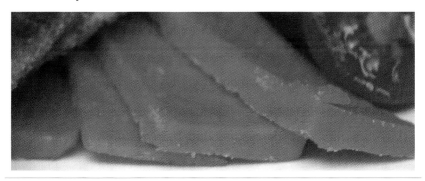

KEY

The marking system used throughout this book is a simple-to-use guide designed to help you assess if you are going to bother making the toastie in question. Provided below is a key to help you understand the thought processes - yes there were some! - behind the marks given to toasties. (For further reading on this subject go to: http://www.triedandtoasted.com)

Taste

0 = Tastes so bad even a rat would turn its nose up at it.
2.5 = This is the middle mark and, as such, indicates the taste is average.
5.0 = The perfect mark. Full of flavour, enjoyable to eat and leaves a warm feeling inside, signifying that a wonderful toastie has just been eaten.

Makeability

0 = You may as well just cook a 'normal' meal
2 = Other kitchen appliances may be required.
5 = No real effort is required!

Final Mark

0 = Don't bother making this toastie. It was 'Tried and Toasted' so you didn't have to!

0.5 = Only make in cases of extreme hunger and desperation.

1.0 = One for the curious.

1.5 = Only for the lack of any other alternative.

2.0 = Worth trying, but only if there is a lack of other ingredients.

2.5 = Can't go wrong with this toastie.

3.0 = A good, solid toastie that won't leave you disappointed.

3.5 = This is a cut above, but nothing to get too excited about.

4.0 = Now we're talking! Probably easy to make and tasty.

4.5 = You need a very good reason not to try a toastie with this mark.

5.0 = A must-try toastie. If you fail to have this toastie before your life ends, you may as well not have read this book. (Obviously, if there is a good reason for abstention, i.e. vegetarianism, please don't feel so bad about not trying it!)

Makeability - This includes any preparation: going to the shop to buy unusual ingredients, pre-cooking and other such things. The higher the figure the less preparation is required. Moreover, how easy is it to make the toastie? If its preparation is time-consuming or at all problematic, it is likely that this figure will be low. The higher the figure the easier the toastie is to make.

Taste - The higher the number, the tastier the toastie.

Verdict - All things taken into account, is the toastie worth it?

Often, the taste and overall mark will be the same, but a toastie should be a simple dish that doesn't require much effort and tastes good. That is why - sometimes - the marks will not be identical. If a toastie takes ages to make and tastes good, the overall mark may not be as high as the taste mark, because it has taken so long to make.

CHEESE KNEES

This is the Ford Escort of toasties. However, just saying cheese is a bit vague. I would strongly recommend only hard cheeses are used. If a soft cheese such as Brie is tried it goes really runny and is likely to make a mess of your toastie maker. I know this because another of my house-share 'mates' thought they'd have a go at a Brie toastie - and left an almighty mess. And I mean LEFT, as supposedly they didn't know how to clean it up; probably true as they apparently didn't know how to wash dishes or vacuum either!

Moving on, be sure you try different cheeses. Mature cheddar is a classic and works superbly for three main reasons: it's hard, melts well and also has a strong flavour. So think of cheeses that have a similar build: Leerdamer, Wensleydale, Leicestershire and the like, all work very well. Stilton, although it's not a 'hard' cheese, works superbly due to its strong taste. The only way to find out what works is to try and toastie it! And don't forget that cream cheese can also be used.

Cheese toastie Ⓥ

In the beginning, there was God and God apparently created everything, including grass, cows, wheat, farmers and Breville. All this makes it possible for cheese toasties to be made ... Amen!

Bread x 2
Hard cheese

Makeability: 4/5
Taste: 3.5/5

"To taste a hand-made, unpasteurised, clothbound Cheddar... is to taste a piece of magic." - J Harbutt, The world encyclopaedia of Cheese, 1998

VERDICT

This is probably the most commonly-made toastie of the lot, and that's largely due to the fact that it is so simple and so good.

Cheese and pickle Ⓥ

St George's day had come around again (April 23 for those not in the know) and, after a day drinking real ale in a country-themed pub, I felt like having a toastie of the patriotic variety. Branston pickle is apparently very British, so I thought that would do the trick.

Bread x 2
Hard cheese
Pickle

Makeability: 4/5
Taste: 4/5

It works excellently, as one would expect from such a classic sandwich.

Cheese and onion Ⓥ

You will only need a slice of onion - use a whole onion and you will be able to make a huge banquet of toasties! Slice some cheese as well and put it in a toastie - easy. Serve with a bit of chutney and some salad.

Bread x 2
Hard cheese
Slice of onion

Makeability: 4/5
Taste: 4/5

VERDICT

A darn good toastie, but don't have it before going out for a night on the tiles. Not only will it unpleasantly taint your breath until the early hours; if regurgitated at a later point in the evening its smell will be undesirable.

Cheese and tomato Ⓥ

This is as classic as they come. Use whatever type of tomato you're comfortable with, just make sure that it is cut up into pieces. If you're using a large tomato slice and neglect to cut it into quarters, you are running the risk of the entire slice being pulled out with your first bite, which can be terribly painful if it makes contact with the skin. On that note, be warned, tomato gets **very** hot!

Bread x 2
Hard cheese
Some tomato
A sprinkling of salt

Makeability: 4/5
Taste: 4/5

VERDICT

Cook two at a time, as you know you'll want another!

Cheese and bacon

They say the smell of bacon is enough to turn a vegetarian into an animal-eating caveman. So spare them the agonising choice between keeping the moral high ground or enjoying a tasty bacon snack by concealing the aroma of this top-notch toastie!

Bread x 2
Hard cheese
Slice of bacon

Makeability: 4/5
Taste: 4/5

The bacon does not have to be pre-cooked; it will cook with the cheese. Cut the bacon into small pieces for it to cook better (one slice of bacon per toastie should do). Serve with some HP sauce or tomato ketchup.

VERDICT

Another good combo, ideal for early mornings, especially the
 mornings after the nights before!

Cheese and corn beef

If only Breville had got around to inventing the toastie maker in time for the Second World War, it would have made eating corn beef a great deal more pleasant.

Bread x 2

Hard cheese

Corn beef

Mayonnaise (optional)

Makeability: 4/5

Taste: 4/5

When World War Three is started by our friends across the water and we all have to live in bunkers underground, connected by a network of tunnels, as long as we have a toastie maker, bread, cheese, corn beef and gas masks, we'll be okay!

Cheese knees

Cheese and ham

When I was strolling through the Yorkshire Dales, I popped in to a tavern for a quiet ale and a bite to eat to recharge my batteries. To my delight the tavern offered toasties - obviously a classy place! - and when I quizzed the rotund landlord about his favourite type, he replied: "cheese un ham," adding, before I could give my approval, "but whole grain mustard must be spread on one piece of bread and tommy K on the other".

A friend of mine swears that the cheaper and more processed the ham the better. One reason for this is that it fits nicely on a piece of bread and therefore cuts down on the preparation required. I find some prepared salad and a handful of crisps complement this meal perfectly.

Bread x 2
Hard cheese
Ham
Whole grain mustard
(Optional)
Tomato ketchup
(Optional)

Makeability: 4/5
Taste: 4/5

    For a quick bite to eat, this is perfect.

Cheese knees

Cheese and mayonnaise Ⓥ

"Chips, cheese and mayo please", I mumbled at 2:30am, after too many drinks in a Derby night spot of dubious repute. As I staggered back home, I reflected on a good value purchase, but the following afternoon it turned out to be an even better buy, as I used the leftovers to make a toastie for 'breakfast'. I cunningly planned to use just the grated cheese remains, but this proved impossible, as they were having a serious bonding session with the mayo! Inseparable as they were, they both went on a piece of bread with another piece on top, and into the trusty toastie machine.

Bread x 2
Hard cheese
Mayonnaise

Makeability: 4/5
Taste: 4/5

VERDICT

The cheese and mayonnaise melt together to form a filling that is stringy and full of taste.

Cheese and egg Ⓥ

There was a time when cooking this toastie would cause a bit of a mess and make me even less popular than usual with my flatmates. But it was worth the abuse, the finger pointing and the having my possessions dumped out of my second-floor window, for this is one lovely toastie. Tomato ketchup and a cup of tea (or coffee) are a marvellous accompaniment.

Bread x 2
Hard cheese
One egg

Makeability: 3/5
Taste: 4.5/5

Another good hangover-cure dish. This is also delicious with MARMITE spread on the outside.

Cheese and orange/pineapple Ⓥ

An unlikely combination that a fruit seller in Portobello market told me about upon seeing my 'So I made a toastie' badge (Who are you calling a dork?).

Bread x 2
Hard cheese
Orange/pineapple

Makeability: 4/5
Taste: 3.5/5

This toastie doesn't add anything to a normal cheese toastie, so don't feel the need to go out and buy fresh fruit especially for it.

Cheese and MARMITE® Ⓥ

One dull morning, the postman delivered me a letter from Australia. It transpired news of this book had spread far and wide and an Aussie pal wrote: "You should throw in some special guest recipes from your mates in Oz. Cheese and Some-other-mite is always a sure winner." So here is a British version, using MARMITE.

Bread x 2
Hard cheese
MARMITE

Makeability: 4/5
Taste: 4/5

If you love MARMITE, you'll love this.

Cheese and peanut butter Ⓥ

I was in a noisy pub talking/shouting with my friends when I was hit with a wave of nausea. One too many babychams? My lunch-time curry toastie preparing to re-emerge at the most inopportune of moments? Far, far worse … it was my round.

"Do you want a drink?" I hollered to a mate on the other side of the pub. "Peanut butter and cheese," was his surprising response. My friends have been guilty of ordering some fairly unusual beverages in their time but liquefied foodstuffs? This was a whole new order of depravity.

Fortunately my pal, unable to comprehend I was offering to buy him a drink, had presumed I was, as ever, on the prowl for innovative toastie recipes, and a healthy dollop of peanut butter with some cheese on top was his recommendation.

Bread x 2
Hard cheese
Smooth peanut butter

| Makeability: | 4/5 |
| Taste: | 4/5 |

VERDICT

I was a bit dubious about this unlikely combination, but it works well. The cheese melts into the peanut butter, resulting in a thick, cheesy, peanut butter toastie.

Cheese and paprika Ⓥ

As I sat in an Italian restaurant, stealing olives for use in a toastie later on that day, a friend from Liverpool eagerly made suggestions for the book. After tediously recycling several ideas I was already fully aware of, he pulled a real rabbit from the hat! "Cheese and paprika ... that has got serious potential," I mused. He was pleased with himself, though naturally embarrassed to be in the company of somebody too cheap to go out and buy olives!

Bread x 2
Hard cheese
Paprika

Makeability:	4/5
Taste:	3.5/5

I used paprika powder for this, which was fine, but don't hold back when putting it on.

VERDICT

Another combination that didn't really add to a cheese toastie. The paprika lost its flavour, resulting in a bit of an anti-climax. Better luck next time my scouse friend!

Cheese and Tabasco or Worcester sauce Ⓥ

Both these combinations work extremely well under the grill, so the question was: Would they translate well into toasties? To find the answer to this age-old question, I cooked a cheese toastie, applied Worcester sauce to the result and consumed with joy and happiness. These steps were followed again, the major difference being that I used Tabasco sauce and drank more water!

Bread x 2
Hard cheese
Tabascor
Or Worcester sauce

Makeability: 4/5
Taste: 4/5

VERDICT

It does work well, and definitely improves the flavour of a cheese toastie. However, the world continues to be gripped by the debate as to whether it is better than its grilled relative.

Cheesy peas Ⓥ

The peas can either be leftovers from a previous meal, fresh, or from the freezer, as they will defrost while cooking. Apparently, cheesy peas are the national dish in Australia and, whereas we have a Sunday roast of beef or lamb, they have a cheesy peas bake. So, how does it work in a toastie?

Bread x 2
Hard cheese
Peas

Makeability: 4/5
Taste: 4/5

G'day mate, fancy another? Yes please, but only on a Sunday thanks!

Cheese and baked beans Ⓥ

Take the two most common toastie fillings and put them in one toastie, it's bound to have good results! A tablespoonful of beans in each side of the toastie will do. Place the cheese - sliced or grated - on top of the beans, add a bit of pepper, garlic granules, chilli power or whatever else takes your fancy, and cook.

Bread x 2
Hard cheese
Baked beans

Makeability: 4/5
Taste: 4/5

VERDICT

Beans in toast with a melted cheese topping: too good to be true? Nope! The cheese really becomes one with the baked bean sauce - very nice indeed.

Cheese and hummus Ⓥ

I can't really remember the thinking behind this one, or who suggested it. I have a feeling I may have had some hummus left over, after trying the hummus and olive toastie. Hummus is very good for you and is generally used as a dip, but can also be used as a filling. It is the Arabic word for chickpea, which gives you an indication not only of where hummus originates from, but also what it consists of (What an education this book is!).

Bread x 2
Hard cheese
Hummus

Makeability: 4/5
Taste: 3/5

Spread or plop the hummus in, put the cheese on top and cook.

VERDICT

This drags the cheese toastie down by half a mark! Try it if you want, but it would be better to cook a cheese toastie and then dip it in hummus.

Snack toasties

Most toasties are of the snack variety, so it may seem slightly strange to have a section specifically for them. However, I simply couldn't think of another way to define these little beauties! We'll start with a filling that is probably the most common after cheese - and that's baked beans.

|| BAKED BEANS

Baked bean Ⓥ

Whenever I'm zipping around my local supermarket, I'm always impressed by the good value baked beans that are available. I'll usually stock up on the very cheap ones, buying at least three tins, safe in the knowledge that this will make roughly 15 toasties; breakfast, lunch and dinner sorted out for five days! A tablespoon of beans in each half should do the trick.

Bread x 2
Baked beans

Makeability: 4/5
Taste: 3.5/5

A solid mark. The similarities with beans on toast are uncanny. You know it's not going to be a great meal but you still love to have it every now and again.

Now what can I have for pudding?

Baked bean and MARMITE® ⓥ

I'm not a particularly well-travelled individual. Venturing from room to room in my luxuriantly upholstered mansion normally provides enough of an adrenalin rush to keep the explorer in me under control. But, on the few occasions I have encountered foreigners, I am always amazed at the unflinching contempt they have for MARMITE. This, I'm sure, is the same for Australians with their MARMITE. Are we the only two countries in the world who enjoy eating this delightful spread?

Bread x 2
Baked beans
MARMITE

Makeability: 4/5
Taste: 4/5

This is a really nice toastie. The MARMITE is full of flavour and goes really well with the baked beans.

Baked bean and waffle Ⓥ

When making this toastie, it is worth putting the waffle under the grill for a few minutes just to soften it up a bit; that's presuming it has just been got from the freezer. Put the waffle in first and spread the beans into the gaps and around it.

Bread x 2
Baked beans
1 Waffle per toastie

Makeability: 4/5
Taste: 4/5

VERDICT

It makes the baked bean toastie a lot more like a meal - polish off two and you're stuffed!

Baked Bean and egg Ⓥ

As with any toastie involving an egg, this has the potential to go very wrong, so be sure you are totally focused on the job at hand. There is no time for wannabes here, this is for the toastie professional and takes years of training and practice. Don't be too intimidated though, it can be done and, in time, will be done. You may be a pensioner by then but hey, all good things to those who wait!

Bread x 2
Baked beans
1 Egg per toastie
(Salt and pepper)

Makeability: 2/5
Taste: 4/5

VERDICT

A good morning toastie, but probably best made when fully awake to avoid a total disaster.

Baked bean and corn beef

There I was, buoyant at having just introduced somebody new to the world of toasties, when my phone beeps with a text message: "Just had a Baked bean and corn beef toastie. Bloody nice, can't wait 4 dinner!"

Baked beans
Corn beef

Makeability: 4/5
Taste: 4/5

VERDICT

Make one and send a text to two mates; in six months the whole country, nay, the whole world, will have tried one! In fact, it would only take about 33 days, with the world populated at around 6,300,000,000, for everybody to have tried one.

SNACK TOASTIES

|| GENERAL

Tuna, sweetcorn and mayonnaise

Feeling peckish on a train journey is never good news. You know, after your knee has almost been removed by the food-cart, that you'll find yourself paying well over the odds for - in this case - a tuna sandwich. I thought I'd make it a tax deductible research expense by saving half of it and toastieing it when I got home.

Bread x 2
Tuna
Sweetcorn
Mayonnaise
Hard cheese
(optional)

Makeability: 3/5
Taste: 4/5

Put the tuna, sweetcorn and mayonnaise into a bowl and mix. Add some herbs and/or pepper to taste and spread evenly with a spoon on a piece of bread. Put the other piece of bread on top and cook in the toastie maker.

VERDICT

As far as toasties go, this is well up there! It's full of flavour and really suitable as a toastie. Try it, I beseech you!

Pizza

Bread x 2
Garlic & Tomato puree
Mozzarella
Another hard cheese
(optional, but worth it)
Slice of onion
Mixed herbs

Makeability: 4/5
Taste: 4/5

Spread the tomato and garlic puree on one slice of bread, cut the cheese into slices and place on top. Finish it off with a sprinkling of onion and mixed herbs anddddddddddd ... toastie! Buttering the outside of the bread adds to the taste, so, if you can be bothered, butter up!

VERDICT

This toastie really works well. It is just a basic pizza toastie; if you want to have pepperoni, tuna, mushroom, sweetcorn, anchovies, or anything else, go for it, it will only add to a good thing. Try using pitta bread too. Either put the filling in the middle (if it will open) or fold the pitta bread over in half. Either way, it's fantastic.

Snack toasties || General

"...although you may be tempted to kiss your toastie machine after it has produced yet another fantastic toastie, this is a flawed idea."

Health and Safety section

Pesto and tuna

When there is no bread in the house I generally suffer a mini-breakdown - what on earth can I eat? I need something that - like toasties - is really easy and tasty. Step forward pasta, tuna and pesto! So how would my backup meal and my staple diet fare when mixed together? A bit of pesto and some tinned dolphin-friendly tuna in between two pieces of bread - simple.

Bread x 2
Tuna
Pesto

Makeability: 4/5
Taste: 2/5

Too salty! These ingredients are clearly best as a pasta accompaniment.

Hummus and olive Ⓥ

This was recommended after a night of fairly heavy drinking. The person in question was just stumbling out of the taxi and was desperate to suggest something - this was the result. Drunkenly, I hailed him as a genius for coming up with such a classic. However, come the next day and the (unusual) luxury of alcohol-free blood, I was beginning to have my doubts. How would hummus take to being warmed up? At least it was easy to make. A blob of hummus in each half and a few olives to match and the snack is made.

Bread x 2
Hummus
Olives

Makeability: 4/5
Taste: 3/5

It wasn't as bad as I thought it might be. The hummus didn't do anything surprising and olives are olives. Try using pitta bread as an alternative to the usual economy bread.

Ainsley inspired recipe

Bread x 2
Basil (fresh)
1 egg
Milk (optional)
Mozzarella
Tomato
Ham (optional)
(Salt & pepper)

Makeability: 1/5
Taste: 4/5

I was flicking through Ainsley Harriet's 'Meals in Minutes' book and found this. It should be fried, so I thought a toastie could also be made of it. It is an eggy-bread (French toast) dish, so preparation is required. Just beat an egg in a bowl, add milk if you want, and then pour into a deep plate. Place just one side of each piece of bread in the plate. While the bread is absorbing the egg, prepare the toastie machine by pouring some oil on to kitchen paper and rubbing it on the plates. This is VERY important! Make sure you cover all the hot plates with oil or the egg will know and stick to any bits you may have missed. Once all that's done, place the bottom piece of bread (egg side down) in the toastie machine, put the mozzarella, fresh basil, chopped tomatoes and ham in, season to taste and put the second piece of egg soaked bread in (egg side up) before closing the machine.

Although this toastie had flavour - without ham, much less so - it was a bit of an anti-climax. After all the preparation and effort it wasn't anything special and is not really worth the trouble. Though I'm sure if it was fried - as it should be - it would be delicious. Isn't that right, Ainsley?

mozzarella-oozing
rosemary ch

ainsley
harriott

ainsley harri

eals
minutes

Cream of mushroom soup ⓥ

After listening to The Velvet Underground, then wandering aimlessly around some art gallery in the afternoon, I had a particular band of soup on the brain. Lethargically carrying out the rigmarole of food shopping later on, I duly spotted some 'cream of mushroom' soup. "Perfect for a toastie!" I thought.

Bread x 2
Tin of 'cream of mushroom' soup

Makeability: 4/5
Taste: 4/5

Just put a spoonful of the thick mushroom soup in either side and the toastie is ready to be made. For extra classiness, add some fresh mushrooms and mixed herbs.

VERDICT

It's like having a mushroom pie, but better, because this is a toastie. Cream of asparagus soup is also very good, as I'm sure any soup of this kind would be.

Cream cheese and smoked salmon

I have to admit that smoked salmon is something I don't have around the place - mainly because it's beyond my somewhat meagre five pounds a week budget - so a special trip to the shop was required! Lay the smoked salmon on the bread, put a blob of cream cheese on top of either side, grind a bit of pepper on top and it's ready to be toastied.

Bread x 2
Cream cheese
Smoked salmon cuttings
Pepper

Makeability: 4/5
Taste: 4/5

VERDICT

Although this is a tasty little number, its expense goes against the whole toastie ethos. Anyway, smoked salmon on brown bread is so nice itself that toastieing it is almost sacrilegious.

Snack toasties

Breakfast is the most important meal of the day, so what better to ingest first thing than a delicious toastie or five? Here are a few suggestions.

|| GOOD YAWNING TOASTIES

English breakfast Ⓥ

I s there a way to make a classic, filling English breakfast, without having to worry about washing the frying pan, the saucepan and the grill - as well as your plate, knife and fork? Yea, yea and thrice yea!

Bread x 2
Baked beans
Mushrooms
Egg
Bacon
(makes it non-veggie!)
(Salt & pepper)

Makeability: 2/5
Taste: 3/5

Put the beans in, then the chopped mushroom (and bacon pieces) and then carefully break the egg on top and season to taste. If the egg goes everywhere, just slap the top piece of bread on and close the toastie maker as quickly as possible.

VERDICT

Either of these will make for a good start to the day. Once you get the hang of the egg trick, it's a relatively simple toastie to make. Best served with a tea or a coffee, and a

blob of brown sauce and/or tomato ketchup.

Why bother?

Tinned breakfast toastie

Uniquely, I found myself having to rise at the ungodly hour of 5:30am. In the knowledge that this would be a long day, I had to eat something that would get it off on the right foot - then I spotted my tin of omelette, chips and beans. My course of action was crystal clear; I had to put this in between two pieces of bread and stick it in the toastie machine.

Bread x 2

Can of tinned breakfast

Makeability: 4/5
Taste: 3/5

A good way to start a long day. It felt more substantial than just having a baked bean toastie and was quick and simple to make, essential factors when you are half awake.

SNACK TOASTIES

Bread Ⓥ

Simple is often good, so why not try a bread toastie? That's right, a piece of bread between two other pieces of bread. The trick is to butter the inside of the outer pieces of bread, sprinkle some mixed herbs in it and you're done.

Bread x 3
Butter
Mixed Herbs

Makeability: 5/5
Taste: 1/5

Verdict

Despite the herb's valiant attempts to liven this toastie up, it's still just a bread toastie!

Garlic bread Ⓥ

It's good to use three pieces of bread as it fills the toastie out. On the bottom piece of bread, spread some garlic puree and sprinkle some mixed herbs on top. Place another piece of bread on top of that and, with the final piece of bread, butter one side and then place on top, butter-side down. Then butter the outside of the top bit of bread and it's ready to cook.

Bread x 3
Garlic puree
Mixed herbs

Makeability: 4/5
Taste: 4/5

This is a fast and simple way to make some garlic bread to go with your pasta meal or pizza. Also, try using pitta bread, either one piece folded over, or just flat, using the middle space.

Garlic bread ii 🅥

This is an alternative version, given to me while I was enjoying some live music at the Kashmir Klub in London. As I sat, listening to the discordant ramblings of Chris Sheehan, a friend of mine came over with what he claimed was 'the best toastie EVER'. Calming me down from my orgasmic frenzy of excitement, he revealed what it was …

Bread x 2 (3 if you want)
Fresh garlic
Fresh chillies
Olive oil
Mixed herbs

Makeability: 1/5
Taste: 3/5

First of all you fry the fresh garlic and fresh chillies in olive oil, then pour this on to a slice of bread and put it in a toastie maker. If you want to use three pieces of bread, I'd recommend pouring the chilli garlic oil onto the middle piece of bread.

VERDICT

A slow and none too simple way to make a garlic bread toastie. Also, oil doesn't react well to being cooked in a toastie machine. My friend has been permanently expunged from my phone book for foisting this upon me!

CHRISTMAS TOASTIE

All the presents have been opened, the port has been swigged, your granddad's falling asleep in front of the TV and it's beginning to dawn on you that you have huge Christmas debts to pay off. However, the end of Christmas isn't all bad, as more often than not there is leftover food, excellent news for the dapper individuals who are partial to toasties.

Mince pie ⓥ

You can pick up the filling for mince pies everywhere around Christmas time. I picked some up from my local 99p shop - yes, everything in it only cost 99p (those trusty £1 shops have been seriously undercut!) - and there was enough to make a classic mince pie toastie for all the family.

Put a tablespoon's worth in each section of the toastie.

Bread x 2
Mincemeat from a jar

Makeability: 4/5
Taste: 3/5

VERDICT

It works! However, I would advise buying some reasonably good mince - the 99p stuff was just too sweet. Serve with a helping of brandy butter, or some variety of cream. Ho, ho, ho!

Stilton and mushroom Ⓥ

There is always some Stilton left over, so why not use it to good effect. Add some chopped mushrooms or pre-cooked broccoli. Slice the cheese and place on the bread; when you start to smell something, that'll be the toastie letting you know it's done.

Bread x 2
Stilton
Mushroom
Broccoli (optional)

Makeability:	4/5
Taste:	5/5

VERDICT

Stilton is a strong flavoured cheese and none of that strength is lost in the toastie. With the mushroom as well, it really is full of flavour. Simple to make and completely delicious, this is what toasties are all about!

Stilton and bacon

Once again we make use of that barrel of Stilton that'll start walking unless it's used. Cut the bacon into small pieces and remove the fat (if you're some kind of health freak!). There is no need to cook the bacon as it will cook inside the toastie.

Bread x 2
Stilton
Bacon

Makeability: 4/5
Taste: 5/5

Yet another Stilton classic!

TOASTIES WITH LEFTOVERS

How many times have you found yourself throwing away
the leftovers of a meal from the night before? Before
consigning them to the dustbin of history, ask yourself
the following questions:

"If I re-heat this, is it likely to result in me getting ill?"
"Would it require an unreasonable amount of force to
close the toastie maker with this inside, between two
pieces of bread?"
"Can I be bothered to cook a 'proper' meal?"

If you have answered no to all these
questions, then you should
consider putting the leftovers in a
toastie.

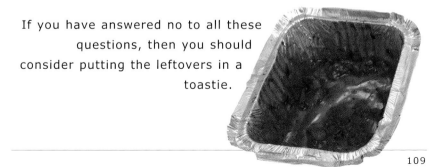

Cheese fondue Ⓥ

Having sauntered around the supermarket, only to find budget restrictions prohibited me from buying anything more substantial than a budget packet of chewing-gum, I returned home to a pungent smell in the kitchen. Was it my flatmates cheesy feet? Worse still, was it my feet? No, no, it was the leftover cheese fondue!

Bread x 2
Leftover cheese fondue

Makeability: 5/5
Taste: 4/5

The texture of cold, day-old, cheese fondue is a bit off-putting, but do not be fooled - it will still be nice. Just put a tablespoon of the hard stuff in each side of the toastie, add a bit of pepper and cook.

VERDICT

Smells like fondue should - which is strong - and tastes great. Try using it in a pizza toastie, or try adding some other ingredients, like onion or tomato, for extra enjoyment.

Noodles Ⓥ

Everybody enjoys noodles from a packet, which cost about 30p from the local shop. Part of the noodle experience is to cup a piece of bread in one hand and fork-lift noodles on to it with the other hand. So why not try some that were leftover in a toastie?

Bread x 2
Leftover 'super' noodles

Makeability: 5/5
Taste: 2/5

There is just no point in doing this toastie. Its only saving graces are that there is a tiny bit of flavour and at least it puts the leftover noodles to some use.

Day-old pasta/curry sauce Ⓥ

Once again, I'd cooked myself a lovely meal, a delightful prawn madras curry, but I'd cooked too much. The next morning I saw the plate there, with a little curry left on it, and did what any right-thinking individual would have done: made a toastie with it!

Bread x 2
Leftover pasta
or curry sauce

Makeability: 5/5
Taste: 3/5
(This may vary depending on who's cooked it!)

This is a great toastie, and one that must be eaten with a knife and fork to avoid any burns on the chin. Simply put your sauce in your toastie, allow to cook, and then eat.

Due to the utilisation of leftovers there is no messing around and this is ideal for the busy, hard working person.

A pitta alright!

Leftover pizza Ⓥ

Cold pizza is really nice, but if you have some and don't want to eat it normally, then try having it as a toastie. There are two schools of thought on this: the first is that the cold pizza is folded over calzone style; the other is that the topping is scraped off and put in with bread, toastie style.

Both work so try them out to see which you prefer; I couldn't really decide.

Bread x 2
Leftover pizza

Makeability: 5/5
Taste: 3.5/5

VERDICT

These are great ways to make use of a cold pizza. The cheese and the flavour all get a new lease of life.

Chips (with some baked beans) Ⓥ

I walked in to the kitchen to see my flatmate had been to KFC the night before (he must have been courting a lady!) and what hadn't he eaten? His chips, the crazy fool! I tucked in to several before it struck me that cold chips really aren't that nice! But there was no way they could just be left lying around, so I made a toastie with them. In one half was just chips and in the other the chips were joined by some baked beans. One side worked, the other side didn't, hence the name for this toastie - the side with just chips in was not great (0/5!).

Bread x 2
Cold leftover chips
Spoonful of baked beans

Makeability: 4/5
Taste: 3.5/5

VERDICT

A good use of cold chips, in fact, it's almost worth leaving some specially! Could work with MARMITE, butter/spread on the outside and/or seasonings on the inside.

Dhal Ⓥ

Dhal is really good for you as the lentils help keep the gut healthy and aid digestion, as well as reducing the risk of heart disease and cancer. It may be perceived as the type of rabbit food only tree-hugging vegetarians would eat, but this shouldn't put you off trying it! It is a tasty dish and tasty dishes always get the thumbs-up. Dhal varies in texture; the kind used for this toastie was quite solid - the really watery variety would be pretty hard to make a toastie with.

Bread x 2
Leftover dhal

Makeability: 5/5
Taste: 4/5

This was really nice. Two of these with some freshly squeezed juice and some exercise later in the day and you're a better person for it.

Spicy bean burger Ⓥ

Oftentimes, as your bean burgers take twice as long to cook in the oven as predicted, you succumb to hunger and tuck in to a delicious toastie to keep you going. And now the bean burgers are done, you're feeling a little full. Well, don't worry, it just means you've got tomorrow's lunch sorted out already.

Bread x 2
Leftover spicy
beanburger

Makeability: 4/5
Taste: 3/5

A good way to make use of those leftover bean burgers. Remember that sauce always goes on the outside of the toastie once it's cooked.

Shepherds pie

Whether it's from a packet or made lovingly in the kitchen, if there is any leftover, stick it in a toastie! There is currently a frenzied debate among the intellectual heavyweights of the toastie world as to how this should be cooked. Should the mash be put in one half and the mince in the other? Alternatively, should each half have a bit of mash and a bit of mince? I'd go with the latter, but it's your toastie, so knock yourself out!

Bread x 2
Leftover shepherds pie

Makeability: 5/5
Taste: 4/5

There's nothing pie-in-the-sky about this!

Mashed potato Ⓥ

Mash is great! Fresh or from the packet, you just can't go wrong with mash, beans, mushrooms, bangers, eggs and toast - it's a classic. However, when I cooked (well, poured boiling water on granules) a packet, with a serving suggestion of four, I really had over done it a bit!

Put a healthy-sized tablespoon of mash in each side. If you want tomato ketchup with it, put it on once the toastie has cooked.

Bread x 2
Leftover mash

Makeability: 5/5
Taste: 2.5/5

There are better things that can be done with leftover mash, like adding some onions and leeks and frying it to make a toad-in-the-hole. If beans were to be added it would push the taste mark up half a point, but basically it's just a bit bland.

Sunday lunch

Sunday is rarely an auspicious day. Not only does Monday follow it, but there is a significant chance a hangover is being nursed. However, in the unlikely event that a big Sunday lunch is cooked, at least you know there may be some leftovers for breakfast, lunch and/or supper on Monday. Get what you can into the toastie: gravy, meat, roast potatoes, veg, and so on. If the toastie maker will close, you're on to a good thing!

Bread x 2
Leftover Sunday lunch

Makeability: 5/5
Taste: 4/5

God bless Sunday.

Toasties with leftovers

"Carefully research what food you may re-heat before doing so. Failure to do this may cause your body to react the next day."

Health and Safety section

Fish fingers

Waking up with some fish fingers is always a nice thing. After a quick sniff and a moment of remembrance, just put them in a toastie. I'd forgotten about mine for a couple of days, and to be honest, I questioned whether or not consumption would result in me getting sick. It didn't, which is why it's here. Put a finger in each half and if you have any beans around, put a few in.

Bread x 2
Leftover fish fingers

Makeability: 5/5
Taste: 3/5

VERDICT

Better than throwing them away. Serve with a bit of tomato ketchup and a cup of tea and you've got yourself a

 classy lunch!

Chicken

It is common to have some chicken leftover if you've gone out and taken advantage of a supermarket deal that week. After hours of cooking, it's a waste to throw it out, so a few things can be done with any leftovers lying around. If you decide to make a toastie with the leftovers, be sure to put some cheese on top of the chicken and add lots of black pepper.

Bread x 2
Leftover chicken
Cheese
Black pepper

Makeability: 4/5
Taste: 3.5/5

Pluck me, it's good!

Shish kebab

I have a Geordie friend who didn't even need asking to try this potentially squit-causing toastie. He assured me it worked and was a good use of leftover shish kebab. Being the heath conscious type he put the meat in the microwave for a few seconds (30ish) just to be safe. Once the microwave had performed it's task, he put the meat on the bread and put some cheese on top of it and it was ready to go.

Bread x 2
Leftover shish
Cheese

If you have any salad and/or pitta left, use it! Apply the chilli sauce on the outside and enjoy.

Makeability: 3.5/5
Taste: 3.5/5

Several days after consuming this toastie, my pal informed me he had experienced no unwanted side effects and that

 he thought it was a toastie well worth

Toasties with leftovers

ROUND THE WORLD TOASTIES

Being an international jet-setter means that one encounters different people from different places far and wide. However watching TV and talking to people is another way to discover that there are other countries in the world with different names like Peru and Molvania.

To enjoy the wonders of some of these other countries through your toastie machine here's an abundance of recipes to see you through!

Haggis (Scotland)

Scotland is one great country; they have given the world whisky ("water of life"), golf, kilts, Loch Ness and caber tossing. However, a lot of this good work is undone by the fact they eat haggis, which is a sheep's stomach stuffed with meat (heart, lungs, livers, etc) and oats. This haggis should not be confused with its animal namesake; believe it or not, a Haggis is also a weird looking, small, three-legged animal!

Bread x 2

Haggis

Makeability: 4/5
(boil-in-the-bag)

Taste: 2/5

Either the haggis can come from a boil in the bag or from a leftover meal. The haggis may be a bit dry so have some red or brown sauce with it (after it has cooked).

VERDICT

As haggis consists of innards which nobody wants to eat apart from the Scottish (and people who scoff cheap burgers!). Save it for Burns Night.

Mozzarella & spinach Ⓥ (Italy)

Pile the spinach leaves (frozen or tinned spinach contain too much moisture and will make the bread soggy) and then put a good helping of mozzarella on top. Sprinkle a helping of mixed herbs over the lot and the toastie is ready to be cooked.

Bread x 2
Mozzarella
Fresh spinach leaves
Mixed herbs
Sun-dried tomatoes
(optional)

Makeability: 4/5
Taste: 4/5

VERDICT

It works really well. The spinach goes soft and melts in with the mozzarella to create a wonderful dish. Serve two-at-a-time with a glass of red wine and some salad.

Vindaloo and naan/chapati ❤ (India)

What makes this really Indian is the bread. Indian bread is just so nice. We may have Hovis and Mother's Pride, but you can't beat a nice piece of naan bread, or a chapati or paratha for that matter. If you happen to wake up on a Saturday or Sunday morning with some Indian curry and bread in your kitchen, thank your lucky stars and stick it in a toastie!

Chapati or naan bread x 1
(from a packet, or a takeaway, or leftovers!)
Vindaloo
(from a jar, or a takeaway, or leftovers!)

Makeability: 0-5/5
(Depending on whether you've cooked everything yourself!)
Taste: 4/5

VERDICT

Either naan or chapati bread works well. Be warned though, chapatis are thin so don't pack in too much curry. Recommended eating for any time of the day. (Also, try some cheddar cheese in a chapati toastie … mmm 4/5.)

Doughnut Ⓥ (USA)

Although it is thought doughnuts were 'invented' by the Dutch (or possibly may have come from the Isle of Wight) then taken to the USA, there is no doubt the Yanks are the biggest doughnut munchers out there! The world record for eating doughnuts is held by an American chap called John Haight, who - in 1981 - scoffed 26 (52 ounces) in just over six minutes. It is also believed Americans eat a staggering 10 billion doughnuts a year.

Bread x 2
1 Doughnut

Makeability:	5/5
Taste:	2.5/5

VERDICT

There is no point in making this toastie. It did have taste, but it would have tasted better without the two pieces of bread. While we're on the subject, if you happen to have a few old, stale or hard doughnuts around, it's worth heating them up in a toastie machine and giving them a whole new lease of life.

Chilli con carne (Mexico)

While zipping around the aisles of my local supermarket, I was attracted to a sign indicating some kind of deal. On further investigation it was a Mexican special, and, after carefully studying my budget I concluded that - for the sake of this book - I should take advantage of this generous offer.

Tortilla wrap
Tin of chilli con carne

Makeability: (3/5)5/5
Taste: 3/5

Most tinned con carne sauces will not be that spicy, so if you're in to that type of thing, pile on the chilli powder or, better still, buy a fresh chilli to cut up and put in. This can be cooked especially for a toastie, or just save some and use the leftovers in a toastie.

Tortilla wraps are thin and burst easily, so do not eat without a knife and fork! Once I'd recovered from finding this out the

hard way, I thoroughly enjoyed this Mexican style toastie.

SWEET TOASTIES

It's teatime in the manor and the maid informs you the scones have all gone, and suspiciously Jeeves has done a runner! What can be had with the cup of Earl Grey? Easy, a lemon curd toastie will do nicely. Moreover, if the pudding supply has all gone, try a tinned fruit and custard toastie. In fact, even if the pudding supply hasn't run out, a toastie is your best bet!

Lemon Curd

Place two good dollops of lemon curd on the area of bread either side of the diagonal line, place the other piece of bread on and you are done. This toastie is an ideal start to the day, or a satisfying accompaniment to ones afternoon tea.

Bread x 2
Lemon curd

Makeability: 5/5
Taste: 4/5

VERDICT

Very good! It goes well with a nice cup of tea or coffee and tastes almost like a doughnut. Be warned, lemon curd gets very hot.

Jam

Put two generous helping of jam in each half on the area of bread either side of the diagonal line, place the other piece of bread on and you are done. This toastie is an ideal start to the day or as a satisfying accompaniment to ones afternoon tea.

Bread x 2
Jam

Makeability: 5/5
Taste: 3.5/5

VERDICT

Good! It goes well with a nice cup of tea or coffee and tastes almost like a doughnut. Be warned, jam gets very hot. Thank God for cut and pasting, eh?

Golden syrup Ⓥ

In my ant-infested kitchen, these six-legged, weight-carrying insects are incredibly drawn to syrup. Little do the minuscule freaks know it will be the cause of their untimely and sticky death! Place two good dollops of ant-free Golden syrup on the area of bread either side of the diagonal line, place the other piece of bread on and you are done.

Bread x 2
Golden syrup

Makeability: 5/5
Taste: 3.5/5

Verdict

Very good! It goes well with a nice cup of tea or coffee. The golden syrup binds to the bread in a way that changes the texture of the bread. Be warned! The syrup can make its way through the bottom piece of bread and become acquainted with the hot plates of the toastie maker, resulting in a very sticky clean-up operation! Don't leave the toastie in for too long.

Fruit dessert topping Ⓥ

If you're feeling particularly profligate - I never am but, like so many, I was given some of this as a Christmas present - then try out this expensive toastie. Place two good dollops of classy fruit dessert topping on the area of bread that is either side of the diagonal line, place the other piece of bread on and you are done.

Bread x 2
Fruit dessert topping

Makeability:	5/5
Taste:	3.5/5

Very hot! It's also pretty tasty too. A great dish to end a dinner party with, it could be served with cream, ice cream or custard, depending on who's at the party.

Apple pie toastie Ⓥ

When tackling this toastie you'll have to go out and buy some pre-made puff pastry. The stuff I used was very good, I managed to get about four toasties out of it. To my amazement, it was more expensive to buy cooking apples than it was just to buy a tin of apples. Whichever you choose to purchase, make sure you add some cinnamon to give the toastie a bit of extra flavour.

Pre-made puff pastry
Tin of apples
Cinnamon
Raisins
Custard/cream/ice cream

Makeability: 4/5
Taste: 3.5/5

Once again, the versatility of the humble toastie machine is demonstrated. The pastry cooks really well and the apple filling gets very hot - all round it's a winner. Normal bread can be used, but it is a nice change to use pastry. NB Also try having some cheese with pastry … mmmmm.

Mixed tinned fruit salad with custard ⓥ

Doctors recommend we should eat at least five portions of fruit or veg a day. So here's one way to achieve that goal; have loads of different fresh tinned fruit in one toastie!

You will want as little of the juice as possible to avoid making the toastie soggy. If you have any of the luxury dessert topping (previously mentioned) stick some of it in here as well. Moreover if you like hot custard put some in with the fruit bits.

Bread x 2
Tin of fruit salad
Custard

Makeability: 4/5
Taste: 3.5/5

VERDICT

I have a shameful confession: I loved school puddings. This toastie was a pleasant reminder of dinner ladies and seconds. Served with hot, or, as I like it, cold, custard. If you don't have custard, this toastie would only score a zero for taste; the bread is noticeably soggy and makes the pudding inedible!

Tinned fruit filling Ⓥ

A nice and easy dish that'll impress the culinary cognoscenti. Opening these tins causes the same type of temptation that cake mix offers, in that you'll be drawn to eat the contents of the tin before it's even come close to the bread. If this is the case, get somebody with more willpower to make it!

Bread x 2
Tin of fruit filling
(Black cherry,
red cherry,
strawberry,
blueberry, etc)
Custard/ice cream
(optional)

Makeability: 4/5
Taste: 4.5/5

Yum, yum! Continuing the school food theme, and doing it in style. Again, have it with custard, hot or cold.

'Eggy bread' toastie Ⓥ

reak the egg in to a bowl and beat. Add a bit of milk and pour in to a plate. Place one side of the bread in the egg and leave to absorb for a minute before repeating this for the other piece of bread. Do not do both sides of the bread (it is not necessary, as only one side of the bread will be cooked). It's essential to oil the plates of the toastie machine as, if this is not done, the egg will stick and it'll take a while to clean.

Bread x 2
One free-range egg
Some milk
Maple syrup/honey/
sugar and lemon/
golden syrup

Makeability: 2/5
Taste: 3/5

VERDICT

Easier than making normal eggy bread, less washing up to do

afterwards and still tasty - everyone's a winner!

Peanut butter and banana Ⓥ

Although my friend and I had suspicious minds about this Elvis inspired toastie, one night we thought it's now or never and made it. The banana can be sliced or mashed, just be sure not to get any stuck on you, as it is such a waste.

Bread x 2
Smooth peanut butter
Banana x 1
(a mini one is perfect)

Makeability: 4/5
Taste: 4/5

This one left us all shook up - definitely do not return to sender! It works very well, so I can see why the King of Rock 'n Roll enjoyed his grilled peanut butter and banana sandwiches with such weight-gaining joy.

Chocolate spread and banana ⓥ

D on't be shy with the chocolate spread, if you're going to be decadent you may as well do it in style. The banana can be mashed or sliced; either way, put it on top of the healthy blobs of chocolate spread and cook.

Bread x 2
Chocolate spread
Banana x 1
(a mini one is perfect)
Coconut flakes
(optional)

Makeability: 4/5
Taste: 5/5

VERDICT

Nice, nice, nice! The banana melts into the spread and tastes just superb! And, in classic toastie style, it's so simple to make - perfect!

Sweet toasties

"To butter the outside of a toastie featuring a chocolate bar could make it quite disgusting and uneatable."

I doughn't believe it section

Mars® bar ⓥ

For those of you with a sweet tooth, this toastie will be right up your street. If friends question your choice of toastie filling and make incredulous remarks like: "but a Mars® bar in bread?", just ask them the following questions: Do you like toast? Do you like chocolate spread on toast? Do you like Mars bars? If they answer yes to all three, you should offer them a piece and watch as they struggle to contain their pleasure. Then offer them a large portion of humble pie. A quarter of a Mars® bar will do per triangle. Much more and it becomes a little bit sickly.

Bread x 2
Mars® bar

Makeability: 4.5/5
Taste: 4/5

VERDICT

This actually works really well, though you'd be hard pushed to have two, as it really is quite rich. The Mars® bar melts and becomes one hot thick liquid. A hot drink would complement this nicely and help with consuming it!

Snickers® bar Ⓥ

I put half a normal sized bar in each side of this toastie. I was slightly apprehensive about this particular dish as I don't like (in fact, hate) cooked nuts, due to a bad experience I had once with a nut cutlet! Anyway, in the name of trying and toastieing, I did it regardless.

Bread x 2
Snickers® bar

Makeability: 4.5/5
Taste: 4.5/5

It was obviously going to be similar to the Mars® bar toastie, but this one edges it because of the nuts. I don't think I'd relish eating more than one, but this was a really nice toastie and it was even mooted that it made a Snickers® bar taste better!

Maltesers® Ⓥ

This odd recipe was found on a website and it was called the 'Maltesers® Surprise'. The surprise was that it - apparently - worked ... I thought I'd investigate this outlandish claim for myself.

Bread x 2
Some Maltesers®

Makeability: 4.5/5
Taste: 1/5

I put three in each half. However you could (if you're in a particularly rebellious mood!) up the ante to four.

A waste of an otherwise great snack, two great snacks in fact, as maltesers® are also a treat! There isn't much chocolate on the little fellows and the bit in the middle goes all chewy. The chewyness actually isn't that bad, it's just the total lack of flavour that is.

TIME WASTING TOASTIES

I've had the pleasure of sampling many toasties while compiling this book, but there have been a few that have been a total waste of time - so bad that they don't even warrant a mark, hard as it is to believe a toastie can ever be anything other then delicious. Obviously, this section has to be kept within reason; a toastie consisting of offal from a sheep, for example, is clearly too grim to contemplate, let alone eat in the name of research. So here are some toasties that failed to impress, or worse.

Crisps Ⓥ

When food levels are low, a crisp sandwich is often the depressing result. So it was only natural to discover how well it worked in a toastie.

Bread x 2
Crisps, any flavour

Makeability: 5/5
Taste: 0/5

It doesn't work at all. I even tried putting a bit of tomato ketchup in one side but it still didn't deliver. As my flatmate observed to perfection, it's like eating small pieces of cardboard! Just for the record, when toastied, popcorn also turns to cardboard.

Tuna and Mars® bar Ⓥ

"**O**h yeah - this is one of those strange combinations that you think won't work, but is actually really nice!" my 'friend' enthused. I was sceptical, but he seemed convinced this was a great toastie, and potentially great toasties simply must be tried.

Bread x 2
Mars® bar
Tuna

| Makeability: | 4/5 |
| Taste: | 0/5 |

VERDICT

My scepticism was well founded! This was indeed a strange combination, and one that didn't work on any level. My 'friend' has since suggested chocolate and chilli, but I won't be partaking after trying this foul concoction.

Avocado and mayonnaise ⓥ

There I am, entertaining some friends, when I bring out a bit of a classy appetiser for us all to eat -an avocado and mayonnaise toastie selection.

Bread x 2

Avocado

Mayonnaise

Makeability: 4/5

Taste: 0/5

VERDICT

The words mushy and not nice spring to mind. These friends don't RSVP to my dinner invitations anymore!

Mackerel in tomato sauce

Tinned mackerel or sardines, with or without the tomato sauce, are a great meal when served with a piece of toast, so I thought I'd try it in a toastie.

Bread x 2

Tin of mackerel in tomato sauce

Makeability: 4/5

Taste: 0/5

As the name of this recipe suggests, I went with mackerel in tomato sauce and it was awful! This was the first toastie I had which made me want to throw up after a mouthful. The problem is that the oil from the fish is released, making the bread soggy on the inside and resulting in a horrible texture.

Baked beans in Quebec maple syrup Ⓥ

These beans were all the way from Canada and that's where they should probably stay. Naturally, they were an immediate candidate for inclusion in a toastie - after all, it's only a slight variation from normal baked beans. However, my expectations were not that high, so it was with some trepidation that I tried it.

Bread x 2
Tin of baked beans in
Quebec maple syrup

Makeability: 4/5
Taste: 0/5

VERDICT

The low expectations were fully justified as I struggled to swallow this awful toastie. I'm not giving minus marks but, unofficially, this has got a minus mark of five. What

 drives me to put myself through such ordeals?

Ice cream Ⓥ

I didn't really think it would work, but this book isn't called 'tried and toasted' for nothing!

Bread x 2
Ice Cream, any flavour

Makeability: 4/5
Taste: 0/5

VERDICT

Predictably, the ice cream melted, went extremely runny and made the bread soggy. This was one of the worst toasties I've had.

Cat food

After carefully selecting a quality cat food, which used gravy and not jelly, and contained some meat, the task now was to find somebody prepared to try it. It took a few months, but after having several pints of Guinness at the legendary Dublin Castle one night, my search was over. A friend was drunk enough and also, importantly, hungry enough, to give it a try for the sake of this book (the things people will do to see their names in print!). So I peeled the lid off, put the cat food in one of the slices of bread, put the other one over and put it in the toastie machine.

Bread x 2

Tin of good cat food

Makeability: 4/5

Taste: 0/5

VERDICT

"It's a toastie I wouldn't have again," Jamie said (the snob!) as he swallowed the last of one half of the toastie. The bread went soggy on the inside and the cat food stank! Only to be contemplated in an absolute emergency.

Time wasting toasties

With thanks...

The following people have helped in different ways, but to all of them I am very grateful for their support and enthusiasm toward this book. Apologies to everybody who has had to endure the endless blatherings about toasties...

The Author cannot close this brief note of thanks without expressing his grateful acknowledgments of the enhanced reading imparted to this little work by Mr. Mark Crellin's editing.